Look After Yourself

Healthy Skin

Angela Royston

Heinemann
LIBRARY

First published in Great Britain by Heinemann Library, Halley Court, Jordan Hill, Oxford OX2 8EJ, part of Harcourt Education. Heinemann is a registered trademark of Harcourt Education Ltd.

Editorial: Sarah Eason and Kathy Peltan
Design: Dave Oakley, Arnos Design
Picture Research: Helen Reilly, Arnos Design
Production: Edward Moore

Originated by Dot Gradations Ltd
Printed and bound in Hong Kong and China by South China

ISBN 0 431 18024 5 (hardback)
07 06 05 04 03
10 9 8 7 6 5 4 3 2 1

ISBN 0 431 18034 2 (paperback)
08 07 06 05 04
10 9 8 7 6 5 4 3 2 1

British Library Cataloguing in Publication Data

Royston, Angela
Healthy skin. – (Look after yourself)
1.Skin – Care and hygiene – Juvenile literature
I.Title
646.7'26

A full catalogue record for this book is available from the British Library.

Acknowledgements

The publishers would like to thank the following for permission to reproduce photographs: Bananastock p.10; Bubbles p.27 (Angela Hampton); Getty Images p.4 (Kaz Mori), p.9 (Colin Hawkins); p.12 (Laura Lane), p.18 (Inc. Janeart); p.20 (Laurent Delhourbe), p.22 (Aja Productions); p.26 (Pascal Carpet); Martin Sookias pp.13, 14, 17; Powerstock pp.6, 8; Science Photo Library p.16 (Dr Jeremy Burgess); Trevor Clifford pp.5, 11, 15, 19, 21, 23, 24, 25; Trip p.7 (Leslie McFarland).

Cover photograph reproduced with permission of Masterfile/David Schmidt.

The publishers would like to thank David Wright for his assistance in the preparation of this book.

Every effort has been made to contact copyright holders of any material reproduced in this book. Any omissions will be rectified in subsequent printings if notice is given to the publishers.

Contents

Your body 4

What is skin? 6

What else does skin do? 8

Look after your skin 10

Keep your skin clean 12

Dry your skin 14

Look out for warts 16

Dry skin 18

Cover up in the Sun 20

Use sun protection cream 22

Cuts 24

Scabs 26

It's a fact! 28

Glossary 30

Find out more 31

Index 32

Words written in bold, **like this**, are explained in the Glossary.

Your body

Your body is like a complicated machine, with many different parts that work together. Each part of your body has a particular job to do.

Skin covers your whole body. It separates your insides from the outside world. This book is about skin and how to take care of it.

What is skin?

Your skin is thin but tough. Skin is made up of two main layers. The top layer of skin is particularly tough.

The layer below contains a substance called **melanin**. Melanin protects your skin from the Sun. People with pale skin have only a little melanin. People with dark skin have lots of melanin.

What else does skin do?

Skin is **waterproof**. When you swim, water cannot seep through your skin into your body. Skin also stops the inside of your body from drying out.

Most of your skin is covered with fine hairs. These hairs help to keep your body warm. When you are too hot, your skin **sweats** to cool you down.

Look after your skin

Skin is tough. You can
cover it with face paint
and then wash the
paint off. Even so,
you need to look
after your skin to
keep it healthy.

You will soon know if your skin becomes unhealthy. It will start to itch or become sore. It may also become dry and flaky.

keep your skin clean

You need to wash your skin to keep it healthy. Soap helps to remove dirt and dried **sweat**. Make sure you rinse all the soap off your skin.

You should have a shower before and after you swim in a swimming pool. A **chemical** in the water called **chlorine** can make your skin dry and itchy. The shower washes it off.

Dry your skin

Dry your skin with a clean towel. Make sure you dry yourself all over, particularly between your toes. Talcum powder helps to get your skin really dry.

If your feet are often damp or **sweaty**, the skin between your toes may become itchy and flaky. This is called **athlete's foot**. It can be cured with special powder.

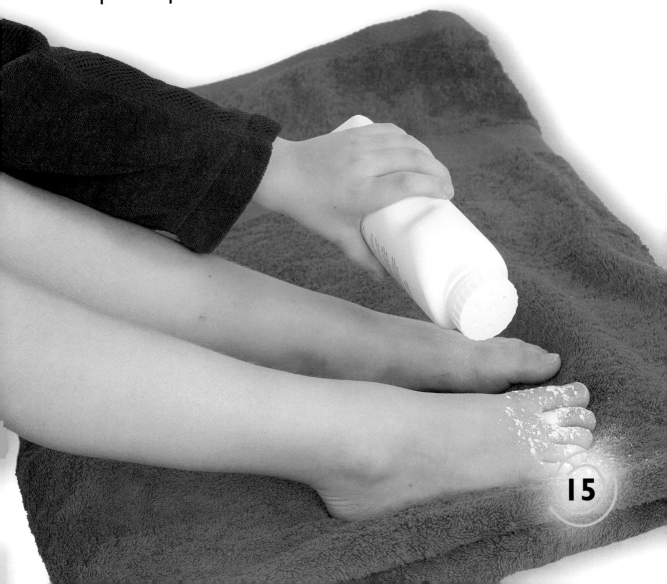

Look out for warts

A wart is a small patch or bump on your skin. It is caused by a **virus**. A **verruca** is a wart that grows on the **sole** of your foot. It can be very painful.

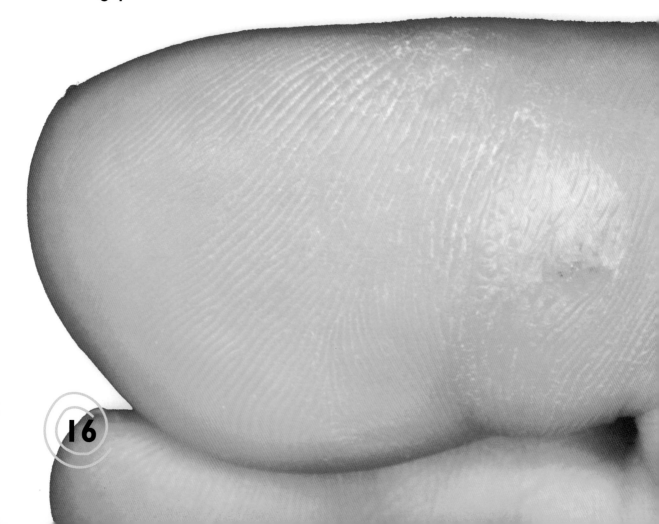

You can get rid of verrucas with a special **ointment**. Cover up your foot if you have a verruca. This will stop other people catching it.

17

Dry skin

Your skin may become dry and itchy if you spend a lot of time in heated rooms. Windy weather can also make your skin dry out.

You can use skin cream to make dry skin feel better, or to stop your skin from drying out. Rub the cream into your skin.

cover up in the Sun

The Sun's rays can harm your skin. When it is hot and sunny wear clothing that will protect the skin on your back, chest, head and arms.

Wear a hat to shade your face from the Sun's rays. If your hair is short, it is a good idea to make sure that the back of your neck is covered, too.

Use sun protection cream

Sun protection cream stops the Sun from burning your skin. Put it on before you go outside. Rub in more cream after an hour or two.

Sun protection cream has a factor number on the bottle. The higher the number the more the cream protects you. People with black skin need to use sun protection cream too. You should still wear a shirt and hat.

Cuts

Skin normally keeps **germs** out of your body. But if your skin is scratched or broken, germs can get in. Help your body to keep germs out.

Wash the scratch in clean water. Blood helps to wash away germs. If the cut or scratch is bleeding, cover the cut with a clean plaster.

Scabs

After a while a hard **scab** forms over a cut or graze. The scab protects the wound while new skin grows. When new skin has formed, the scab falls off.

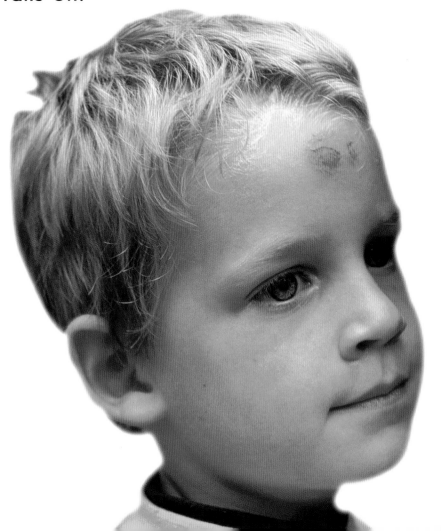

Do not pick scabs. Wait for them to fall off on their own. If you pull off a scab too soon, the cut may start to bleed again.

It's a fact!

Your skin contains tiny **pores** that allow **sweat** to escape from your body. Most of your skin has up to 100 sweat pores in every square centimetre (that is an area about the same size as your big toenail).

Some parts of your skin contain more sweat pores than other parts. The skin on the palms of your hands and on the **soles** of your feet has a lot of sweat pores. It is important to wash your hands and feet to remove the dried sweat.

The top layer of your skin is made of tiny flakes of dead skin. Washing helps to remove the dead skin. Millions of these flakes rub off every day. In fact most of the dust in your home is made up of flakes of skin!

Pale skin burns more easily than skin that contains a lot of **melanin**. People with pale skin have to be particularly careful to protect their skin from the Sun.

Some people have **eczema**. Patches of their skin become very dry and itchy. Special cream can help to make the skin less dry. Eczema cannot be passed from one person to another.

You may sometimes get a **rash** on your skin. Your skin becomes red and covered with small spots. Many different things can cause a rash. An **allergy** to something, such as a food or soap, can cause a rash. Some illnesses, such as chickenpox and scarlet fever, also cause a rash.

Glossary

allergy   when the body reacts to something as though it were a germ, although the same thing is harmless to most people

athlete's foot   disease that makes the skin between your toes itchy and flaky

chemical   substance, for example chlorine, which is put into the water of swimming pools

chlorine   chemical that is added to the water in swimming pools to kill germs

eczema   when a patch of skin becomes dry and itchy

germ   tiny form of life which causes illness

melanin   brown chemical in the skin that protects you from the harmful rays of the Sun

ointment   creamy solid that usually contains medicine. It is rubbed on to the skin.

pore   small opening in the skin

rash   many small red spots on the skin

scab   when a blood clot forms a hard covering over a wound

sole   underside of a foot

sweat   salty water that the body makes in the skin

verruca   wart that forms on the sole of the foot

virus   type of germ that can easily pass to other people

waterproof   does not allow water to pass through

Find out more

Safe and Sound: Clean and Healthy by Angela Royston (Heinemann Library, 2000)

Well Being: Physical Well Being, My Skin by Joy Cowley and Enrico Sallustio (Folens, 2001)

Why Do I Get Sunburn? by Angela Royston (Heinemann Library, 2002)

Index

athlete's foot 15, 30
cuts and scratches 24, 25
dark skin 7, 23
drying your skin 14
dry skin 11, 13, 15, 18, 19, 29
eczema 29, 30
germs 24, 25, 30
hairs 9
itchy skin 11, 13, 15, 18, 29
melanin 7, 29, 30
pale skin 7, 29

pores 28
protection in the Sun 7, 20, 21, 22, 23, 29
rash 29
scabs 26, 27, 30
skin layers 6, 7, 28
sore skin 11
sweat 9, 12, 28, 31
swimming 13, 30
washing 10, 12, 13, 25, 28
warts and veruccas 16, 17, 30
waterproof skin 8